.

For Noelle, my sister.

Although I still can't put my grief into words,
losing you has awakened something in me I never knew I had.

I love you.

Edited by Angelo Colavita
Cover: Liza Corbett, *Floralia* (2017)

ISBN 978-0-9995558-3-5
Copyright © 2019 Arielle Tipa
First Edition 2019 Empty Set Press. Philadelphia, PA, USA
www.emptysetpress.com
Printed at Fireball Printing. Philadelphia, PA, USA
www.fireballprinting.com

daughter-seed

arielle tipa

EMPTY{ }SET
PRESS
PHILADELPHIA

i'm painting a hatred of you   1

Little Burdens   2

safe connect   3

zephyros   4

Secondhand Haunted Macaroni Necklace   5

night-blooming   6

index of rarely seen flowers   7

the circumference of salt   8

( )   9

orphan seeds   10

daughter - seed   11

slightbirth   12

a likeness   13

a likeness, pt. 2   14

Baby Robot™   15

———   16

III   17

index of rarely seen flowers, pt. 2   18

my wormwood   19

this place has everything my god it does   20

i'm painting a hatred of you

my twin, my twitch —
prettily you demonstrate your lazy eye
the rococo latticework of your scapula —
you are most beautiful in braille
my hammock, my summer
my opium glitch, my tambourine din
i've been cat-tongued in places you have never lived
in tantrums you have never nursed
you are killing me to death —
my ictus, my itch

Little Burdens

We live beneath the shadows of our skirts. Every day, we survive on baby food smoothies and sore-throated kumbayas. Warm temperatures make us cough. We write obscenities on our unicorn wallpaper and we are healthy and beautiful and good.

But Mom doesn't like what we do. She doesn't like when we go to that closed down gas station and break the windows. We pretend the broken glass is diamonds and we play pirates. Our pirates are allergic to diamonds. We stuff the diamonds in our pockets and wonder why our hands are bloody.

Mom scolded us for making coffin shoes out of boxes with dead hamsters and our little neighbor cried. We play games and pretend we are carousel horses, neighing *Befit me, befit me. Am I your favorite color? Are my teeth bared enough? Befit me, befit me.*

We hold prayer circles at night when the stars smell like something burning. With arms outstretched, we can hug an entire continent.

We are healthy and beautiful and good.

safe connect

i am somewhere today

the crook of your arm maybe
under a bridge, nestled in your collarbone
or the blueprints of a chandelier, a mention

please deserve me, i am childless and a child
i have forgotten my mother tongue and i
can only speak in acronyms and bad omens and clicks

and the sounds you make when we place a candle
at the end of every diving board, under every bridge

zephyros

my dear,
you are not venus —
your gilded oyster shell
is a five-by-three foot walk-in tub
with its encircled evidence
of rose-pink glycerin soap
and your hair cannot
cover, drape
the delicate pearl
between your thighs

that man outside
your lofty
motel window
will not entreat you
to a lust-scented
expiration
of west wind

he's carrying
a brown paper bag
and praying to a street light
on his knees

Secondhand Haunted Macaroni Necklace

He leaves his hiccuping saddle next to a drainpipe that's drooling for a parking fee. Promises to carve my name into every split tree from a car crash. Walks with his eyes closed when it's windy and has nine fingers and an affinity for sharp objects. Googles how to violate a rosebud with tweezers. Buys signal torches on the darkweb, passing them off as fireworks. His agnostic prayers are small enough to fit inside a violin. Unblessed. Sick. An achy bellyful of plums and sugar. The seasons pass in reverse when he yawns.

He approaches me, wearing his finest kitsch items to ward off evil.

night-blooming

everywhere
the harvest flies can hear us
deep-six in rhythm

with our needlepoint   kinetic

to the shock footage

of breathing   only seen

in higher plants

index of rarely seen flowers

unsex me so good i'll glitch botanical
a vanishing so delicious i could drink it

unlove me so hard i'll break delightful
so pin-up and princess i could cry

unkink me so fast i'll turn wretched and rascal
i'm dying i'm drooling it tastes so good

the circumference of salt

waist-deep in the spasms of my spine // i calculate // the folklore of warm saliva // the musk between our legs // the potential of raw almonds // flesh // all pink and soft and yours // of heavy cream in sewer pipes // the slippery alarm of frightened fish // so says

my tongue // graceless // neck-deep in the contortions of a cherry stem // so goes // the circumference of salt // the radius of our cuticles // a litmus of peaches // of tree sap // so ends

// our appetite

( )

i am full of children i do not want

clumsy and fingerless, i melt from your bell sleeves
i swallow you in teaspoons, unpregnant
a void of pink apples and swollen from salt
oh my hush, my baby sugar, my ghost-white and beloved
i can smell you with my sex

and i am fingerless like your bell sleeves

orphan seeds

please   uproot us at a gentler pace
have a look-see at our precious increase,
our bed trauma

eat from us our all   and
stitch us back to sleep

daughter - seed

hello permafrost jubilee // muck in my gut // babysugar // all cramps and kitten tongue and gooseflesh and houdini wine // you stillborn catcall // you hiss

muck-in-my-gut // ghost-white and beloved // give me a disregard for neighbors and sirens // give me a glass of old and pretty and expensive // give me buttery hair and a nosebleed // give me crawlspace in your warm undress

hello gut-muck // hailbine // pull-down // cursed cuscuta // diwali garland // hello spring

slightbirth

flies obscure our perfect vision
and   ignore the wounds

we kindly offer,
the smallest of caul we clean   each spring

leg-wise
we are fawn   and bambi oozing
and our amnion leaves us,
fresh as day

a likeness

half-love,
>i have become sticky sweet, afterbirth
>hieroglyph and vintage ache, grandmother toad
>a tattoo of surrender dorothy

    love,
>i have bottled and buried you in schist
>in my undergrowth, unshaven
>in my splendidness, my silhouette

a likeness, pt. 2

/

doubt

never have i ever undressed with my eyes closed
or mourned in a color other than #3B3C36

//

doubt wears saddlebag hips,
uglier than christ child in renaissance
doubt is a bird's nest on each shoulder,
hatchlings kept warm in the syrup of when / if
doubt breathes backwards in a rabbit panic, a nosebleed

///

doubt

i have decoded your hex, your fetish sub rosa
i have learned your language and it is mine

Baby Robot™

<< one ♥-shaped button short of a christened gaze, microchips in psalms ‖ pink computer watches her owner (i.e. girlchild) use a crinoline as a birdcage ‖ sends email sans afterthought, subject line: *may I suggest Viagra.jpeg for your condition?* ‖ (the dial-up signal is an Amber Alert) ‖ girlchild, web-diary entry 5/13/03, is curious as to why her Speak & Spell didn't sound like the wet nurse ‖ accidentally tells the waitress *my condolences to the chef* in appreciation for her chicken tenders and twice-thick chocolate shake ‖ covers pink computer with Lisa Frank stickers only to realize they weren't glow-in-the-dark, like the package said ‖ a sledgehammer to the circuit boards (chemicals, heavy metals, *precious metals*), she welcomed a new gender ‖ from the trash heap, pink computer could still feel girlchild's stomachaches, ~~a suicide hotline for cravings~~ an embryonic telephone call >>

_____ reads mobile tarots because she's afraid of getting a papercut.

Always disregards her daily horoscope and is infallible to prophecy.

She has the demeanor of spoiled milk and the complexion to suit it.

Hisses back to every cat on the street.

Always mistakes the letter *A* for the number *4*.

Always sells paint color samples to children in the back of her van
      in broad daylight.

_____ disguises herself as a blind animal, saying her name is *dog*
      spelled backwards and a creamy synonym for *dying*.

Always slices cake with rusted scissors and always ends up dropping
      her honeyed dates onto her thrift store carpets.

_____ always ends up eating them anyway.

She has oily roots and a temper, asking herself if she's even worthy of
      a shower.

III

I walk as if the world has robbed me of a favor. It's getting late and I head into the woods where there are bears. Bears smell blood and so I turn myself into a boy.

I succeed in laying my head on my lap and I realize I was born on a Tuesday which means I will die on a Tuesday. There are MISSING posters taped to trees for children who look like their pets. Slowly, I remove one with the picture of a girl who looks like a dog I used to own. I keep it.

The trees are littered with underwear and there's a candle right next to me. The sun is almost up and so I decide to hold a séance for past lives and all of my imaginary friends show up. They hand me something round and I say:

I want enough money to buy love

I want enough love to make money a thing unwanted

But the magic 8 ball only tells me "reply hazy try again".

I want enough confidence to seductively lick a knife

This time, the ball tells me "ask again later".

I wonder what it sounds like to die. The sun is up and I sneeze into the crook of my arm where there is now evidence of the séance and I feel dizzy. There's a woman who smells like a bonfire of windchimes and I tell her I don't believe in the devil. I realize the woman is a bear and I bleed heavier this time.

index of rarely seen flowers, pt. 2

hag baby, my little spit

i am very full of water
and bad skin and paint samples
with names like milkworm, bone china lily
violet bitter, weeping madonna
glinda in repose

some things of you i try to disremember:
the aftertaste of your touch, your abdomen glow
brightest and birdlike

you'll burn more delightful
and suffer with me

my wormwood

seedling
sapling and gingerbread thief
behold the ickyness of my orifice, my anatomy

      the half-moons and cyanide
      i can't ungag
      the nightpills, the sleep
      so itty bitty

            my coccyx flower
            my dear and doomed
            i reek of you, i remember you

this place has everything my god it does

and everything is so beautiful everything is organized by color and clarity and price and sickness.

tantric chocolate. herringbone flags. an ankh-shaped paperweight. hemlock shampoo. an automaton. jinxes. this hedgehog can do your taxes. marie antoinette's snuffbox. jolly chimps. don't watch vic morrow's death scene. phantasmagoria. crystal pepsi. the metaphysics of a bird. a free download.

tell me good baba is there a spell for this i have one shekel one lira one rupee and bottlecaps and my hair is oh so soft oh please.

i am silkworm tender and ziegfeld glowing and stew-worthy everything is making me so so soft.

i am darling electric and tulip fever and floating and gone and everything is so beautiful i want to cry.

Several of the poems in this collection
have previously appeared in the following journals:

Vagabond City	*i'm painting a hatred of you*
Grimoire	*Little Burdens*
FIVE:2:ONE Magazine	*zephyros*
DATABLEED	*index of rarely seen flowers, parts 1 & 2*
Millennial Pink	*Secondhand Haunted Macaroni Necklace*
SHOW YOUR SKIN	*the circumference of salt*
L'Éphémère Review	*( )*
Dream Pop Press	*daughter - seed*
FADED OUT	*Baby Robot™*
Really System	
Rag Queen Periodical	*III*
Sad Girl Review	*my wormwood*
Breadcrumbs Mag	*this place has everything my god it does*